HEIFETZ *Collection*

WITCHES DANCE *(Le Streghe)*
for Violin and Piano

NICCOLÒ PAGANINI, Op. 8

Critical Urtext Edition

Edited by Endre Granat

KEISER

EDITOR'S NOTE

Niccolò Paganini's (1782-1840) *Witches' Dance* begins with a quasi-operatic Introduction followed by a Theme and Variations. (Theme by Franz Xaver Süssmayr).

A mature work of Paganini, it uses all the innovations the composer introduced: double stops, three and four part chords in rapid successions, harmonics in single and double notes, left hand pizzicato, scales and arpeggios using the entire range of the instrument. This work, like so many others by Paganini has not been published during the composer's lifetime.

This Critical Urtext edition is based on the very first edition of the work. Jascha Heifetz' bowings, fingerings and his suggestions regarding interpretation are integral part of this edition.

Endre Granat

WITCHES DANCE
(Le Streghe)
for Violin and Piano

Violin

Critical Urtext Edition
Edited by Endre Granat

NICCOLÒ PAGANINI, Op. 8

HANDEL PASSACAGLIA FOR TWO VIOLINS *ed. Stephen Shipps/ Endre Granat*

Outside of his native Norway, Johan Halvorsen (1864-1935) is known internationally only for his arrangement of Handel's Harpsichord Suite. The Passacaglia is performed as a mainstay of Duo programs in his arrangements for both Violin/Viola and Violin/Cello. Jascha Heifetz established these duos in the standard literature by playing and recording countless performances with William Primrose and Gregor Piatigorsky. **HL00126549—S512002**

WIENIAWSKI POLONAISE BRILLANTE NO. 1 (Polonaise de Concert) *ed. Endre Granat*

In 1848, the thirteen year old Henryk Wieniawski wrote the first sketches to his Polonaise in D major. The composition was published in Germany in 1853 as *Polonaise de Concert in D major op. 4*. When the work was re-published in Paris (1858), the title changed to "Polonaise Brilliante". Tremendously popular already during the composer's life time, this work has been on the repertory of virtually every virtuoso violinist ever since. This new Critical Urtext Edition corrects obvious misprints while keeping the format of the 1853 first edition, printing the textural changes on the Paris version as foot notes. **HL00141930—S511020**

WIENIAWSKI POLONAISE BRILLANTE NO. 2 *ed. Endre Granat*

Completed at the zenith of Wieniawski's career in 1869, this virtuoso piece showcases the playing of many fast, short and accented notes on one bow stroke which came to be called the "Wieniawski staccato". The slow midsection in F major contains some of Wieniawski's most lyrical themes while double stops and trills conclude this irresistible work. The signed and dated (1869) manuscript found its home in the library of Jascha Heifetz. As a member of Mr. Heifetz's studio, editor Endre Granat studied this work with the Master. This Critical Urtext Edition is based on this manuscript and the first printed edition (Schott 1875). **HL00126550—S511019**

SAINT-SAËNS INTRODUCTION AND RONDO CAPRICCIOSO *ed. Endre Granat*

This work was originally intended to be the rousing Finale to Saint-Saëns' First Violin Concerto, op.20. Saint-Saëns' favorite violinist Pablo de Sarasate gave the first performance in 1867 in Paris with the composer conducting. In 1869 Saint-Saëns entrusted his younger colleague Georges Bizet to create a reduction of the orchestra score for Violin and Piano. The composer's autograph score and the first edition of the work were the primary source material for this publication. **HL00141931—S511021**

SAINT-SAËNS HAVANAISE, OP. 83 *ed. Endre Granat*

The composer dedicated this work which dates from 1885-87 to Rafael Diaz Albertini, a violinist of Cuban origin. This Critical Urtext Edition is based on the composer's manuscript, the first print of the violin and piano version, and to a large part, on the historic recording by the composer himself with the violinist Gabriel Willaume (1919). **HL00141932—S511012**

THE JASCHA HEIFETZ BEETHOVEN FOLIO *ed. Endre Granat*

Contains Heifetz' *Three Cadenzas to the Beethoven Concerto for Violin and Orchestra in D Major op.61*, along with the Beethoven violin solo with piano works, *Turkish March op. 113* and *Chorus of the Dervishes op.113*, both from *The Ruins on Athens*. All works in the collection are Critical Urtext Editions by Endre Granat. **HL00145437—S511024**

BAZZINI LA RONDE DES LUTINS (DANCE OF THE GOBLINS) CRITICAL URTEXT EDITION *ed. Endre Granat*

This great bravura piece uses many of the innovations the composer learned from his teacher, Niccolo Paganini--ricochet and flying staccato bowings, double harmonics, left hand pizzicato, and repetition of the same pitch on all four strings. This work remained one of Jascha Heifetz' favorite encores. He recorded it in 1917 and again in 1937. His bowings, fingerings and his suggestions regarding interpretation are integral part of this edition. **HL00153335—S511025**

PAGANINI WITCHES DANCE (LE STREGHE) FOR VIOLIN AND PIANO OP. 8, CRITICAL URTEXT EDITION *ed. Endre Granat*

A mature work of Paganini, Witches Dance uses all the innovations he had introduced as a violin virtuoso performer. Like so many of his other works, it was not published during the composer's lifetime. Jascha Heifetz' bowings, fingerings and suggestions regarding interpretation are an integral part of this Critical Urtext edition by Endre Granat. **HL00153336—S511026**